WILL YOU WALK A LITTLE FASTER?

Penelope Shuttle has lived in Cornwall since 1970, and the county's mercurial weather and rich history are continuing sources of inspiration. So too is the personal and artistic union Penelope shared with her husband, the poet Peter Redgrove, until his untimely death in 2003.

Her first collection of poems, *The Orchard Upstairs* (1981) was followed by six other books from Oxford University Press, *The Child-Stealer* (1983), *The Lion from Rio* (1986), *Adventures with My Horse* (1988), *Taxing the Rain* (1994), *Building a City for Jamie* (1996) and *Selected Poems 1980-1996* (1998), and then *A Leaf Out of His Book* (1999) from Oxford Poets/Carcanet. She has since published four books with Bloodaxe, including *Redgrove's Wife* (2006), shortlisted for the Forward Prize and T.S. Eliot Prizes, and *Sandgrain and Hourglass* (2010), a Poetry Book Society Recommendation. Her retrospective, *Unsent: New & Selected Poems 1980-2012* (Bloodaxe Books, 2012), drew on ten collections published over three decades plus the title-collection, *Unsent*. *Heath*, a collaboration about Hounslow Heath with John Greening, was published by Nine Arches in 2016. *Four portions of everything on the menu for M'sieur Monet!*, a pamphlet, was published in 2016 by Indigo Dream Publications. Her latest collection, *Will you walk a little faster?*, was published by Bloodaxe in 2017.

First published as a novelist, her fiction includes *All the Usual Hours of Sleeping* (1969), *Wailing Monkey Embracing a Tree* (1973) and *Rainsplitter in the Zodiac Garden* (1977).

With Peter Redgrove, she is co-author of *The Wise Wound: Menstruation and Everywoman* (1978) and *Alchemy for Women: Personal Transformation Through Dreams and the Female Cycle* (1995), as well as a collection of poems, *The Hermaphrodite Album* (1973), and two novels, *The Terrors of Dr Treviles: A Romance* (1974) and *The Glass Cottage: A Nautical Romance* (1976).

Penelope Shuttle's website: www.penelopeshuttle.co.uk

PENELOPE SHUTTLE

Will You Walk
a Little Faster?

BLOODAXE BOOKS

First published 2017 by
Bloodaxe Books Ltd,
Eastburn,
South Park,
Hexham,
Northumberland NE46 1BS.

www.bloodaxebooks.com
For further information about Bloodaxe titles
please visit our website or write to
the above address for a catalogue.

Supported using public funding by

**ARTS COUNCIL
ENGLAND**

Cover design: Neil Astley & Pamela Robertson-Pearce.

Printed in Great Britain by Bell & Bain Limited, Glasgow, Scotland, on
acid-free paper sourced from mills with FSC chain of custody certification.

For my family and my friends

ACKNOWLEDGEMENTS

I am indebted to the following journals, e-journals and anthologies in which some of the poems in this collection first appeared: *Artemis, Best British Poetry 2015* (Salt Publishing, 2015), *Hwaet! 20 Years of Ledbury Poetry Festival* (Bloodaxe Books/Ledbury Poetry Festival, 2016), *Ink Sweat and Tears, Magma, Her Wings of Glass, Ploughshares, Poem, Rewiring Histories, Southbank London, Stony Thursday, The New Humanist, The Dark Horse, The Manhattan Review, The Poetry Review, The Rialto*, and *The Yellow Nib*.

Some of the poems in this collection first appeared in the pamphlet *In the Snowy Air* (Iota/Shots, Templar, 2014).

I am grateful for a grant from the Arthur Welton Foundation to assist in the completion of this collection.

CONTENTS

My Life

My Life, I can't fool you,
you know me too well,
I'm sad of myself,
days live me in vain,
you test me
but bin my answers,
you're so busy, so tired,
evenings in the glass,
drink them, My Life,
but you won't,
driving your bargains
of years gone by,
promising me
this and that till
the walls are spells,
the roof's a star,
and
I seal the hour
in a tear,
a mortal tear,
I know you so well,
My Life, not at all

Hvallator

You could live here forever
on Hvallator
without easy chair or clock,
plainsong of the four winds,

why not live here forever
on Hvallator, especially at low tide
when the beach is collected by hand,

wolf evenings
when you sing as you sew
down-lined comforters for the clergy,

you can live here forever, can't you,
it will keep the father quiet for hours,
tales of Imperial Russia at his beck and call,

wolves and foxes at home on Hvallator,
little green island, pressed flower of an island,
ten thousand dawns you will see, on Hvallator,
the voes at midnight shining like silver gauntlets.

Quiet Year

My quiet year begins,
a month of fairchild days,
I'm not worn out by them,
quiet cloud after quiet cloud

Then comes a month
of spendthrift days
in quiet shops,
a maze of buy-me-now scarves
and salsa shoes,
days of turning pages
in a whisper of wordcounts,
but not a dropped pin to be heard

My quiet year...
However hard you listen
you won't hear my heart beat,
or my heart breaking...never hear this house
when it sighs. How quiet is quiet enough?
No one knows, this month or the next,

footstep month
measuring the coastal path,
quiet green highway
above the half-heard sea,
surf rolling quietly in
towards my birth month,
month of silent spells, cast,
month of silent nets, cast,
fishing up days quiet and days quieter
than you believed possible. Spider
in her soundless web, sound waves
hushing like fools

Every night you sail closer
to the wind, all month long
listen to whatever quietness you please...

Sometimes quiet fills the house
in the guise of a smoker's ghost,
rescue is not guaranteed,
this may be your least favourite month

But in the main
this quiet goose-girl year suits you,
you're happy and sad,
nothing needs to be said,
choose any time of day or night
for not saying a word,
not even in the month of rainy days
when the rooms fold in closer,
there's nothing they can't bear... And you?

My quiet year has nowhere to go
but here and there,
drifting from weather
to weather... time for me
to meet another month
on its own silent terms,
adjusting my silence to fit

The year turns, remembers
how much it has lived through,
heart in mouth,
quiet moon surging quietly to the full,

leaning to its darkening
in a darkening month,
full of pity
for those on the brown...

Month of stars and toys,
not quite enough quiet to go round,
memory's bee hum
in winter, not expected, accepted...

A new year...
but don't start flying round the world
like Diaghilev's lost citizenship...
Remember that slumbering line
of lorries you saw
in the early off-road dark
not a million miles from Gatwick?
Why not begin this new year
with a silence like that,
or with the folk-land silence after *Firebird*'s blaze,
or the quiet of the dice
rolling your fate towards you across the baize?

Demons talk in the air

Demons talk in the air
all the time
(like)
men crossing and criss-crossing in mid-air high-wire melancholia
(or) mirrors coming down from *there*
(full of) passing strangers

On each pillar (mirror)
smiley mouths (asking you) to step inside

There's gentle car-washing music,
you can hear it equally everywhere

Mirrors keep (coming down)
        like demons
with black numbers pinned
to their eyes,

asking (you) to step in,
watching and hissing and washing the car

Sometimes it makes you feel watched
in this world of steel
(and) hanging portent
while

someone else keeps buffing their motor
(till) it shines
like a round dance round the colour red
(too big) for its boots

Summer has no lover

but the bee
who lives rent-free
hard to believe I know
but true
so smile on their love
summer has no lover
but the bee
who squares the circle
across England
and Wales
my word how hot the days are
my word how close the nights
can this be
because summer
has no lover but the bee
who simmers through the toasty days
in cahoots with his shadow?
Give me your hand
let's turn tail
on summer and her bee
does she really love him
give me your hand
over the drought-white hills
and the dusty river beds
its up to us and no one else
how far we go my lovely
give me your hand
lend me your ears
let's be gone
let's be done with love
and love-struck summer
and her blessed bee

The Penelopes

I saw *The Penelopes*
painted and named
but not shamed
on a brick wall
along Calvert Street,
Banksy-esque
I guess,
unsigned urban art,
two young women
on horseback,
en-face.
Though I had my camera
I didn't take a photo,
cameras lie,
they blunt and flatten,
but I kept the white Penelopes
in my eye,
a few days later
it seems
in my mind's eye
they rode on elephants
or camels or elands,
any creature but horses,
and I wonder if I go back
to Shoreditch
(but it won't be tomorrow)
will the Penelopes still be there
drawn by an easy clever hand
low down on a wall
on Calvert Street?

Chagall

His father was a merchant of herring
his mother's shawl wraps the child
Moishe went to shortened schooling
fell in love with Bella
the jeweller's daughter
off they buzz to the hive of Paris
his father goes on carrying heavy barrels
earning 20 roubles a day no more
no word will ever ease my father's load
why leave Vitebsk son
city made of wood snow on its roofs
fish in the clouds violins in the blue
a violinist of the twelve tribes
seeking the stars
why son?
Pappie don't be sad
Moishe dreams the bible
he goes to paint the Patriarchs and the Heroes
he's solemn and chatty with some angels
he's brother to the light
understands colour
like a beggar in the park where the circus
pitches its heart but years years find
stars clouding round the dead souls
here's the desert
heaps of boots clothing
ash dung
painted David descends to him
harp in hand
he wants to help your son weep and recite chapters of Psalms
and remember how
buttered bread was never out of his childish hand

Prayer Diary

(for Alyson Hallett)

Today is the day
the 54 bus prays for all
who live or work in Henleaze

the day
when those who can
pray for those who can't

when the unhappy
pray for the happy

the blind for those
with twenty-twenty vision

today is the day
trains pray for the auld lang syne
of their passengers

birds pray
for the good luck of the sky

hearts pray
for the steady hands of cardiac surgeons

the day my dentist
prays for the health of my teeth

      alas he must pray harder
      for a piece of tooth has just broken off
      into my breakfast granola

today is the day
bookshops and libraries
pray for their readers

and villages pray for the cities
who shut their ears alas

when I pray
for all those women not found
by the 1911 Census of England and Wales

and bulls pray for the Ceramics Gallery
in the V and A
        pray for the empty vessels

and when the day murmurs –
just let me get through another bloody day

today is the day
when prayer has been prayed

now burn the midnight owl
for a bit

now sleep

Will You Walk a Little Faster?

Like Rosamund the Fair
I speed over Folly Bridge

like Alice
I look both ways
before crossing Speedwell Street

I'm not
as you see
an official guided walking tour

Like Fair Rosamund
I quickstep down Rose Place

like swift Alice
I skip across St Aldate's

the brainbox city
huffing and puffing in my ear

I'm not hurrying off
to visit a dozen harpsichords

or the church
where William Morris was married

or to see the remains of a dodo
I plan to read

not one
of the six million books

in the Bodleian
or admire a single dreamy spire

or stand in sombre silence

on the spot

where Latimer
Mortimer and Ridley
were roasted alive on god's turnspit

because I'm heading straight
for the heart

of this leather-bound city
where's there's good reason for shadows

where I'll find
panaceas of lavender

penny-royal and nettle
rose-petal potions

medicinal oak-scented valerian
balms and syrups of hollyhock

daffodil and milk-thistle
the Many-Leaf Pharmacy where

like the porpoise not the snail
I'm walking a little faster

waltzing like Rosamund the Fair
and Little White Alice

through the wards and waiting rooms
of The Physic Garden

earthy source of tincture and tisane
the help-yourself of nature

who wears a green coat
not a white
don't you agree?

Heart
I think of

the deep clap
and swoosh
of its workings
strange heart
where the blood lives

When I gaze at my heart
I see not much there
but dark
it is a mystery
no open book

and often
my heart joins me at night,
a visitor I might enjoy
if life
were different

'Knowledge'

My one knowledge
is all I have
it comes back to me
however I travel
lends me an ear
exhibits me
the affordable art
of clouds and rain
I love my one knowledge
more than I can
or should
a whereabouts
neither of good or evil
my one knowledge
reading me
bookwise all day
spider-weaving me
homeless all night
drinking me up
jeroboam by sparkling jeroboam
till I'm lost
to the battlehorn –
oh my! oh my!
it's a wise street
that knows its own postcode

Encounter at the Shrine

You can ride the shrine bus,
it goes all about,
says a frumpy devout one,
we nod and smile
but don't take the bus,
nor follow the trumpeting signboards –
this way Confession
this way Holy Water –
but drift towards the exit
where again she finds us –
Ah but you're going the wrong way,
the shrine's over there –
so we say thank you,
but we're for Knock Airport
in the hour,
ah, she says again, keen-eyed,
good-hearted,
fumbling in her bag
with home-made mittens,
then I'll find ye
a card each,
they've been touched
to Teresa's holy bones –
but her big woolly hands
won't obey her,
give them your spare cards,
Cathleen, she says to her friend,
and I'll settle with ye later,
so the three of us
are given prayer cards
touch-blessed by the saint-bones,
and bidden dear farewell,
back we go to the car park,
through the ranks of shrine matrons,
shrine maidens
and their silent menfolk,

less at ease now in our secularity,
this time we don't mock
the empty plastic bottles in the shape
of Our Lady, ready to be brim-filled
with holy water,
nor do we flinch at the sight
of further kitsch in the kiosks,
the unbreakable Mother Teresas
and rosary skipping ropes,
but go blessed on our way
to the airport of the pilgrims
on its sheared-off mountain top
and gladly gladly
do each of us shell out
our ten euro airport development tax
to the benefit of the good cause
which is Shrine Management.

Quiet Street

Dwell-time
along the quietest street in London,
no one speaks
of the death of the walnut tree.

Footfall time
along this quiet street,
a woman waits in her kitchen
for her husband to go to the tennis club
so she can read Paradise Lost
aloud to herself.

Put an island on my breakfast plate
the day I turn wise,
plus the deeds to a diamond mine
in the back of wherever,
be kind to me like that.

Down-time
along this quiet London street,
time to remember
his eagle's grip on happiness,
trees in Richmond Park,
the sky's lovely struggle with light,
a day full of too many days.

Walking the Walbrook

(for Tom Chivers)

Where's the Walbrook
   gone long-gone
      under Calvert Street

under Tokenhall Yard
   under your stepping feet
      under wells

banged-up in their cells
   under a circus or two
      sans animals save

a few stone lions
   in old Bethlem's once-garden
      Fin's Bury

Where's the Walbrook
   buried alive
      under silts and gravels

Wale-broc
   stream of the strangers
      there are paths below this path

tracks and trailways
   goat paths roman paths
      pilgrim paths

stacked high
   one upon another
      When the road higgles up

or bobs downhill
   the Walbrook's
      calling the shots

down there under London's
      falling walls
            that rise again

in the Eastern Cluster
      as architecture plus money
            The Pinnacle

The Helter-Skelter
      The Walkie-Talkie
            The Cheese-Grater raking it in

Where's the Walbrook –
      rivery ditch long-gone
            by Rivington Street

choked to death
      under Tivoli Corner
            Boy Court and Little Elbow Lane

hung out to dry
      under Scalding Alley
            Three Needle Street

and Number One Poultry
      (that hellhole on high)
            the great stone bully

Cannon Street Station
      Our wet-clay churchy city
            has had its rivers

and lost them
      Some will be found
            others never retrieved

If you shiver
      as the growly snow flurries up
            you're walking

over the river's grave
  through twists
    and turns of an ancient city

its blue afternoon
  laid like a smouldering hand
    on the glass flanks

of great towers
  who never dream
    a river lies at their feet

    hounding them

river no one will ever
  restore to the light
    river long-gone

like Mithras
  under stepping foot
    under plaza-champagne bars

(yet hard to stop
  a river flowing
    under the Bank of England...)

The table at Leacroft

No one spoke
of anything but the war
even though
the war had ended
seven or eight years ago –
the dead whirled round
my young life
as real as the living –
they leaned out of the sky
pressed on the world
dark forces at work –
but I was used to it
expected it
everyone talking about the war
swallowing the sword of it
at the tea table on Saturdays
the dead pushing and shoving

Major Titov Orbits the Earth

6th August 1961

I'm fourteen
a girl I suppose
but a possessed one
I don't care about Gherman Titov
orbiting for the Motherland
far above me in the blue
I'm possessed
spell-torn
my first poems
bucking and kicking
like unbroke colts
words rocket me
into my own outer space
accelerations
to inner worlds
Word-stung and wild
I'm oblivious to danger
from that day to this
at full gallop
one flesh with myself
bloodtrue it seems
(was it? is it?)
in the sanctuary-trap of words
no way back
and not caring about Major Titov
up where there's no space garbage yet
From his tincan craft
Gherman peers
down the well of air
sees his own smile drift
back up to him
from oceans and deserts
while I write my way
a girl I suppose
through the spinning day

my feet not touching the ground
even when the Major
makes safe landing
in the longlost (is it?) USSR

Modis

At first glance
our planet of the silver lining
looks idyllic,
morning-glory-blue planet,
thousand mile curve
of a white cloudbank rearing up
like a Hokusai wave,
beautiful floating ice tongues,
watersheds of the far northern latitudes,
blood vessels of Nile, Ganges,
Yangtze,
the Katanga Delta
twisting like a whirlwind,
the Amazon luminous
and ragged as time-torn lace,
clouds of Storm Isaac lit by moonlight,
local midnights, the tiny blaze of Rome,
dawn like a travelling shrine
speeding the continents,
but look closer,
we're in snow-melt season,
storms of the arctic summer
rip off vast swathes of sea ice,
shoving them to warmer sites,
by 2020 the sea ice will be history –
at the same time
we're in the season of wild-fires,
springing from their home forests
across Russia's Far East,
fire and smoke
over Siberia, Tuva, Tomsk,
Yakutia, Krasnoyarsk Krai,
along the coastline of the Sea of Okhotsk,
dozens of red spots photographed
by Modis the satellite,
the all-seeing,
while on the other side of the globe,

the Mississippi is a mud-trough,
its waters at a record low,
almost one hundred ships
carrying coal,
grain, iron, steel –
flies in the spider web of drought.

No matter how beautiful
this planet looks at first glance,
it has no silver lining,
two great storms
are moving towards China,
one making landfall south of Shanghai,
the other north of Shanghai,
simultaneous storms are never good news,
a vast dust cloud blows westward from Africa,
heads south at Cape Verde, then
turns north, passing over the archipelago,
travelling on
across the Atlantic
to South America and the Caribbean Sea.

Seen by satellite
the earth looks like the work of great artists,
Turner, Claude, Picasso,
but all these colours
drifting seductively across the planet
are how the climate looks
when it's changing,
racing on smoky winged feet
across Russia and Australia,
our broken planet
spinning and scheming,
drowned fathom five
under ice-melt,
or burnt-out like the Mohave,
the one place on earth,
incidentally,
which resembles the planet Mars
more than the red planet itself.

Anchor

The anchor
is a ship's will of iron –
knows there are 1800 storms a day
any ship might bow before –
daylong lightnings
bolts striking
up to forty times a minute –
the anchor
       every flake of rust
       every forged link
is a hold-faster equal
to the storm
Just as sixteen million cattle in Texas
herded by helicopter
are unafraid of 'copters
lordy thars jist our farmer up in the sky
so the anchor is fearless
of gladiatorial combat
between iron and element
       bring it on
as the ship bucks and boings
in the lashed haven
The anchor's chain clatters
when lowered
like a strong vow renewed
and I think the anchor
not the engine
is the ship's heart also
the links of its chain
the very vessels of blood-flow
holding ship to seabed
as love is held to its fidelities –
so praise the anchor
the chain and the hawser
for even when laid-up in dry dock
the anchor is never entirely off duty –

look down from the wharfside
wonder at this David of iron
undefeated by any Goliath of storm and gale

Tales

(for Dennis Lowe and Julie Foley)

Teller of tall tales
comes to my little house
whirls me away to Helston
and its navy larks
then to Tuscany
where we're up a tree
with Massimo
who's got wine and a huge joint
watching through lovely dope-haze
a nightful of badgers
rats and foxes
walking about below us
snuffing the earth

Teller of tall tales says
we're present and incorrect
everywhere everywhen
little-pup moon above
three-mile-high angels
protecting
life and limbs of us
keeping mountains safe

Teller also has tales of Vegas
and all those talking statues
he's wrapping me up warm
in his big stoned embrace
as the student clowns and acrobats
ride home to Penzance
in their class A sub
and old Falmouth days of life
rain down on us
who were there
forgetting
we've lost everything and nothing

I often think

or feel
I'm still inside
the heart
There I am
I come and go in there
I look as if I'm outside
the heart
and everything's upfront
and ordinary –
But no
I'm
inside the heart
making the most of it
in spite of everything
coming and going
with my Kindle
my password
and my shopping

There's no time to think twice
only time to know
I'm inside the heart
where its Thursday
at least one day a week
and I'm getting closer
and closer
to you
despite what people tell me
is the otherwise
but they don't know a thing
about this heart
of ours
do they
and what it can do
without even trying

As I fell

As I fell I woke
I sang I spoke
pain for a breastplate
nothing for my breath
I kept thinking
about Henry VII
and his account books
but that's enough about me –
there are all these days
to be numbered
these journeys
to be fulfilled
As I fell
it came to me
it was only my life
folded into silly solemn minutes
of years
and for every thought I had
there was another one
I couldn't hold
close enough to think
and these
un-thought thoughts
were my downfall no doubt
my bad habits
and my mark on the page
for suddenly I couldn't sign my name
being unlettered
strange to relate

On the ceiling

The dead are writing on the ceiling
but the surgeons don't look up,

the dead are writing
all sorts of interesting things

on the ceiling,
but dear dead people, why use invisible ink?

The dead are writing on the ceiling
as if their deaths depended on it,

if you squint up
maybe you'll see some of their words

flickering between this world
and the next,

the dead are writing about life and death,
but the cardiac teams won't look up,

they keep dragging the death away,
then the dead grab it back,

float up through the ceiling,
free at last

Streets and their childhoods

Town propped by a river
streets and their childhoods
coming and going
cloaking and uncloaking their eyes
my own shadow plucked from me
by old hands of the past
or by the river
never trusting me again
The great Heathrow planes hang
as if by magic in the unclouding sky
their big-angel shadows go
over street and field
steely shadow-wings whisking
over paths I took
in the leaf of spring
door to closed door
along the drifting byways
as if never to be seen again
by the eyes
or even the eyes of the heart
      oh well
old hands of the past
breaking everything to dust
so life is not this or that
fair or foreign or forlorn
old skimping hands
busy about their business
I come and go
the riverside streets
where I was a chidden child
in mesmeric dusks
of old old town
clouds are soon full of dark
voices of strange word
songs in cold blood
memory's silver spade

planting its ceremonial tree by the river
but it can't be done
this looking back
the past a sort of telling not to be heard
it mustn't be done
this act of putting heart or soul
into the old cruel hands
that cloak and uncloak time
till my true life far from here
maybe never happened
but what shall happen now?

Along the great moon

Along the great moon
comes brassbold dog-tired day
looking for a fight
driven and drifting
by the great everything-is-mine moon
what the eye remembers
is a tear is it?
what the ear recalls
the hand that stung it?
what the street remembers
isn't true?
(that's true)
Along the great moon
comes the bus brandishing
its red tongue
the river standing for nonsense
The Shard
lovely lovely *loverly* Shard
goal of all urban climbers
(Alain Robert's nabbed from the building
before he...)
The Shard
glass mast of tallest sailing ship
steeple-singer
jumped-up one
vertical thinker
multi-use Shangri-la
moon's bitch

In the snowy air

The street caved in
showed us old scars
flood-level treasures
a trinket in the form
of a gladiator's hand
coins, tokens
bone-pits
The street caved in
it had too many years
to carry
            here you take them
but everyone flits by
perhaps from shame
at the poor street's plight
or fearful of the counting houses
made of glass more
immortal than mortal
if you lean your head back
stretch your gaze up
at the blinkless glass
of Broadgate Tower
and the steely sky beyond
it will make you cry
I promise

In the snowy air
the old city flies
here and there
its rivers near and far
streets paved with bone
old city
flies through the snowy air
without a care
No one calls its tune
streets are its secret lands
it climbs the black steps

to the terrible plazas
to clown-ugly Number 1 Poultry's
roof-garden of boundless pain
where one who splunged
to his death
fell with champagne glass in hand
in the year of our lord 2007
watched by the ghost
no doubt
of St Benet Sherehog

    2007
    there goes nothing

The towers bear
huge daft names
The Pinnacle
The Shard
The Walkie-Talkie
they're not free to roam
they want the sky
all of it
but they're on their own
and hard to love
the smart clubs darken at last
Boundary Street
counts its ghosts
no one can come back to life
in the old city
where the towers pitch up
through icy air
thinking they're immortal

Old streets
of the passing city
are where I fought
to be alone
friends for shadows
fire-doors flat with terror

Darkhouse Lane
and Three Needle Street

In the snowy air
bones of the city
are a choir for me
less or more
bones in their vault
on Curtain Street
reburied here as the road-engineers
and aldermen decreed
the bones did not rise up
someone blessed them
into their new charnel
where London's little road
turns a sleety corner
and here's a garden
bare as a knife
fountain for drinking
iron cup on a chain
let's look where we are
and count the bones of
no let's count the gates
of London
including the seventh
that never existed
in London
where I'm not sleeping
you notice
sleepless
as the snowy air
of the early hours
or late

Easy Street

Once upon a time
I knew a pupil and a teacher
but they're gone now

no good
panning the heart
for the gold of them

The world
thinks it will live forever
like a wise man's wife
but the world's wrong

On Easy Street
no one lies awake all night fretting
but there are never any houses for sale
along that street
no sirree

My father promised me a sword

My father promised me a sword
his voice leans
like sleet
over loch and mountain

father of me
lone-wolf father

(I knew I must line
my scabbard
with sheep's wool
to keep the sword-edge true)

His voice roams me on
salt in my wound
days blue and obvious as veins
nights in the towns of dust and clay

My father
cups me in his word
weighs me against blood drop
grain of rice
and hath-thirty-days

The sword dims in my grasp

iron blade
and jewelled hilt
scorn the hand
of their making

     A doom of rooks
     in throat-rough parliament
     above the old grave at St Hilary

My father
of the sleety air
my father of his silence
his sword of stardust
and ash
as years go by   as if he'd never been

The Same Coat

The dead follow rules too simple
for us to comprehend

Like a dragon of seven hurts
my dead friend turns from me

The dead are like an ancient type of Christ
they all wear the same coat
my friend wears it the dark strange coat

my friend my friend
who loved to see Fuji or Osaka
painted on a fan

Carry

No one can carry
the tune
that sings
the first beat of dusk
No one can remember
how much they earned
in their dreams
or how they carried
a priceless spoonful
of mouse blood
from ward to ward
patient to patient

no one can do these things

My Arthurian Heart

My heart
tries me on for size
then discards me
like a sleep too ordinary.
I don't know how
to please my heart
or where to bury it.
But that's academic,
my heart's untouchable,
flush with ransom payments.
Or my heart's a lunatic
mistaken
for a wedding guest
who knows life at sea
ain't all scrimshaw and rum.
My heart worries me
from one end
of the Round Table
to the other,
dog with a bone,
heart in its shriven shrine,
heart of Guinevere
or Merlin,
no longer mine.

Early

Yesterday
was an Alfred Wallace day
tilting out to the shoals
off Mousehole

Today's
the outskirts of London
quiet as a mouse
where
in early light
I fear no evil
of a day
like
the kind thoughts
of a friend of a friend

Day of a day
listening to its thought
skimming
and scolding along
memory's melting ice-shelf

The boats go out
three or four
early tide out of Newlyn

That was yesterday
I'm not there
watching
but here
where London
almost begins
where the Thames
goes along broad and deep
to Runnymede

where this room
lets the minutes tumble
along
and
books of many tongues
are quiet

not their moment to speak

The world's a long way off
a radio too faint to hear

No thoughts in my head
I haven't thought
ten thousand times before

I can't bide my time forever
so I glance at my life
as it goes by
lived and unlived
strange
skimped
dipped in time
where I'm the day's watcher
left for dead or love
in the green world's eye
when the river blows
the May horn
so loud it can't be heard

Costa / Henleaze

Where the day goes
might be Henleaze
or elsewhere
sunlit and strange –
breakdown vans
and fire engines on alert
passers-by dreamy
with their shopping

footfall true to itself

Where the day goes
no one's the wiser
for the buses
change their route numbers
as often as you change your mind
so where we'll end up
is anyone's guess
going where the day goes
in Bristol by the sea
where the idleness of any person
discovering a fire
can only be wondered at
and taken home
to be recorded
carefully
before the day slips
out of grasp
and the cold cloudless night
comes back
and all the electric blankets wake up

little monday

(for Linda)

little monday
from the very beginning
all of me waking
to the first big artics
swinging round the roundabout
starry with lights –
shock of local time
little monday
here there and everywhere
getting in the way –
several kitchens share
the same space
we all set to work
the living the dead
2000 nightingales
and old Monet
in his painted garden
little monday won't end
but that's not right
it must
so the stars can wake
or else stop spinning
says Einstein
in the everyday of my ear
and I was a gazellope again
skidding between
one Elvis moment and another –
strange to be this same person
all these years
putting my hand in the fire
learning nothing
knowing I'm worth my weight
in sackcloth somewhere
worth my weight in starlight somewhere
but not here

no not here
what was I thinking
at a minute to dawn
on little monday
or is it omday

Both Hearts

This heart liked the day
and that heart
liked the night
but both hearts
liked ciggie smoke
and Chanel No 5
as they groaned
as they clung
this heart without a care
that heart
with time to spare

First heart knew everything
but so did second heart –
made itself
into a crystal ball –
asked first heart
to gaze into its cold sphere
Other heart said:
things I see there
are never all I see
are they?

First heart loved
rock 'n' roll nights
jet-black blood-red music
squaring out
of The Electric Ballroom
but second heart
wanted the silence of scrying

This heart liked bread and water
but so did that one

Often
I couldn't tell them apart

London, December

I only love London in winter

MONET

Daybright city darts in
        for an evening paper,
                comes out dark-savvy, neon-wise...

Trace the city
        in your tilting eye, river
                cocking its snook through the post-codes,

idling past fiscal towers,
        great see-thru slabs of executive toffee,
                shrugging off this faff of a city without a second glance

as one rose-red bus
        half as old as time
                wheedles its way down Threadneedle Street

and bridges lie low for fear of burning
        and a million mobiles raise
                their homebound voices

and forests of Xmas trees,
        chopped off at the root, encircle London,
                closing in...

Once I knew a man
        who wished his house
                had two magical doors,

one leading to London,
        one to Cornwall –
                'think of the travelling time we'd save...'

But London, my love,
      has so many doors
            all hitting the nail on the head,

London in its mysterious cloak of dark
      not much darker than the light,
            city where a painter

can only work on his 'Crucifixion' canvas
      when he's blind-drunk,
            yes, that'll be London, I think

Dear Shard,

I've watched you
from day one
growing Babel-high
a world-wonder from the train
and all around
the clouds love you
as much as I do
they cradle your tall head
pillow your young eyes
now you're the finished thing
unexpected
from all angles of London
piercing skyline
eye-line
as if you're jumping
from here to there all the time
London Bridge to far miles away
how do you get yourself *there* I ask
so in love with you
I can't spell my own name
I love you Shard
from the hotel in your shoes
to the red beacon that glows
at your shardish crown
like god's ever-lit bulldog-breed cigar

City wakes

to its time of life
roofers
clouting the air awake
clouds wrong to begin with
then right
city wakes in wrath
and SpongeBob trousers
scoops river up
like a bag of thrones
old churches
run for their lives
waking city
lives at the crossroads
plain for all to see
from where do you come?
seeing-eye streets
go in and out of harm's way
among the seven acts of mercy –
what a long time they've been alone

Poor London

People of the poor London
fast-shriven

in the blood-boltered ways
of men

The slain bus
flinging hands and eyes
into a Bloomsbury everywhere

City fast-shriven
in its ways –

under a back-slidden river
a broken train

whirling round itself forever
in the smoky-dark tunnel –

eyes hands legs

In my heart

On days when I live
in my heart
its not easy
there's too much there
that rules me and eats me
and bears me
as its child to the world

On nights
when I live in my heart?
so many tears
and crocodiles
and little drinking horns

Architecture students
of course
come for a *peek*
at my enormous
vaulted domed heart

When I live in my heart
then I *live* in my heart
that's the rule
it seems
my heart snazzing me round
in its gale force 12 tabernacle tent
or like Tate Modern on a roll
with all that restless shipshape *shape-shifting* art

Of course
there are days and nights
when I don't live in my heart

times when I'm strangely *heartless*
strangely *unborn* in a slapdash way
all mossy burial chamber/*not* heart

my honeydew snail-catching blood
circulating quietly
when I'm not
living in my heart

But then again
there are days and nights
when I live in my heart
and nothing's easy
and no one can help
and I don't know
the worst of it yet
          do I?

O blinde Augen

My voice
my voice alone
will touch you
from crown to heel
a glass of Siberian champagne
downed in one –
As the storm takes the coast
to its breast
my voice will bring you back
our vanished day –
As the sea surges over the freeway
my voice will flow to you
on bended knee –

My voice will tend you
like a child raised by wolves

All this is true
and now
I will tell you one of my lies
            beloved
as I used to
and you always understood

'O blinde Augen / blöde Herzen!' [O blind eyes / stupid heart] sung by Iseult,
in *Tristan and Iseult* by Richard Wagner

Little Bus

Route 35

The little bus
buzzes
through the backlands
workplaces
and farms
a wooden house here
a breezy bridge there
steep and turning hills
wind-y narrow road
making cars
reverse
and respect the bus
respect
there's that apple tree lane
we used to park up by
the gate with the iron dove
daffodil or cabbage fields
the stony path
to Maenporth
the unforgotten years
are there
and the end of them
that's there too
the bus skirmishes on
through Bareppa
where the flock of geese were
long ago
now I see one
by the stream
then we press on
to Helford Passage
where the river
tugs at its own heartstrings
to this very day
          if you get my drift

Passages

A circle of moons
holds the year in place,
silver-green moon year
where April is four o'clock,
May is five o'clock,
a circle of moons
runs the earth to ground,
there's 'a sort of magic
made out of circles and colours'
where time meets the seasons
without fear, green is a sign
of caution unfenced,
part of the fiery
and outward beauty
of a seven-day painting,
April is four o'clock,
May is five o'clock,
the world goes up
into the mountains to see
her fortune,
scorch marks of the sun,
but who turns the tallest mountain
to face south,
the only eye-witness a shadow?
Sunset reads out an apology
from biblical times,
ghosts and heroes are the same,
the soul goes on dreaming after death,
the living and the dead each have a star,
the lackey moth spins
its grey-gossamer chrysalis-tunnel
over the thorn bushes on the cliff

*

A dozen Weymouth Streets
converge on the stroke of noon,
the living quiet can't be found
in this fool of a London,
go to the green woodland
that knows its own mind,
the long shear
of the beechen
stepping down the western shore,
go where the walled garden
of summer sails to and fro,
read aloud the salt time-table
of the tide,
and if this time next year
I'm still sleeping
in the smoken city
where red is my swain
and blue the sister of my soul
it's no one's doubt but mine,
no one but me
pushing my hands and foolish feet
into the fiery streets.

*

Mandalas of immediacy,
'visionary cartography',
the disc of Los, golden wheel,
shining spokes
in the shining hand of Los
as he begins his shining journey
through the circular world
of which there are many vision maps,
mappae mundi and mandalas,
and at the world's leathern edge
there's an eight-armed man
who walks about
in the Siberian woods,
there are dragons

I don't really know,
here's another map of the world,
a wheel that never turns
or touches the dust,
a map of cities and wary beasts,
rivers and labyrinths
and unsleeping saints,
a map as of old, geographies
of beast and child and stone,
a turning world
of turning seasons
holding the year in place,
push your hands into its compass,
Blake's North at your feet,
his South at your head,
his West your circumference
by day and night,
his East your centre, you are
gravity's child,
Icy Hell is a pink rose,
the world turns
painted on a bough-wheel,
melancholia is the moon,
the flower, Jerusalem,
the sun bright between golden wheels,
the world turns,
a ship's wheel, a compass,
small red glints of railway roses,
wildings, a blue map now,
oceans and clouds and skies,
cog of the entire,
lost cities looking back at the world
through pilgrim spectacles,
a map made of hands and feet,
not mine,
cog of the entire,
the reflective traveller
has many maps,
a map of Alicestone,

map worlds circling and spiralling
round the days and nights,
a map of mountain walks for artists
and romantic people,
but the unmapped world
is ever at hand,
beware, London is also a Wolf,
wolfhead and big blood claws,
wolfish river, babel towers,
so much howling...
turn to the map of the parchment soul
painted to show
where Los lives,
he holds the burning orb
in his true hands,
he might go from York to Durham,
who knows?
from Ely
to an unknown town
that stands forever upside-down
on the banks of its river...

*

London asleep,
shorelit shore of rain and blowy air,
harbour born
to be rich and brazen,
London in its full-length sleep,
parklands rolling on like billows of the sea,
even the little parks,
Lee Valley, Watling Chase,
White Webbs, Railway Fields,
a city not lubberly, sea-dog city,
mermaid city, Sabrina fair,
her watery tresses wrapped round Wapping
and Highgate,
Seven Sisters and the Caledonian Road,
roadmaps of rain,

queenly wet city in her green rags
of wrecked June,
waterscape city, juniper city
thorny with bridges, sacred loneliness
of old age,
winding history round a little gnarled finger,
the colour-house by the Wandle,
Sunday city rolling back and forth,
pebble in the strandline,
pirate city wharfed and lost,
found and lost, treading the balance bar of fortune,
riding its turning wheel,
shut-eye grey-ghost city
born to be wise and scatty,
Sunday morning quiet as a razor
gleaming on a captain's table
in a cabin in London in its stormlit shorelit dawn,
Neptune rising from the deepest deeps
of steep morning mirrors of London quiet
winking back at the vagrant of itself,
unfurling snarling pearl sails for a broken-mast morning...

*

...unread watch-face of 5 a.m.,
an asleep city opens and closes its gates,
clouds roll over in grunty sleep,
rain stealthes about neither here nor there,
shop windows blink, show off blingy dreams
to no one,
escalators keep moving,
who knows anything about their metal hungers?
A sleeping day yawns itself heart-first into the hour,
steps towards the light
that bodies out for miles and miles,
fierce and forlorn is the working day,
along channels and groynes
of the roads and trackways
a rushing serpent of people

swallows the city
as they are being swallowed by it,
city of turning spits of rain,
the multi-tongues of the city wagging
and wishing and cussing,
voices summoning a million lattes,
a million flat whites,
a million frappaccinos,
she talks in Clapham Junction Costa
of *how in the time of Jesus*
we have a different view
from what we can read in the Bible...
Bread and dust, clouds and river,
goldfinger banks of toil and trouble,
towers, bridges, subways
leading from the light
to the light via stinking dark,
longing falls on its own deaf ear,
a sermon of sorts
slams itself into silence,
and the people around are fine about this
but
Why do the people not come
in the church on Sunday
as they do in my home? And when some
few come prayers and choirs are automatic,
how is that for you?
Miles of the city pace
back and forth
in their own lost time,
the city throws the dice,
fortune slams the door, is she in here with you,
or has she left the building?
I'm different person
from whom I appear,
I can't be with them honest

*

The living
and the dead
of the city
each have a star,
living and dead
know their place,
the living and the dead
keep a garden of the self,
a sort of lovely inner poverty
in the city
that balances out
the desolation…

What to do about the heart?

What to do about the heart
was a constant problem

the ribcage hanging there
like a bony birdcage

when the bird's flown

Everyone had a different idea

about the heart
and everyone looked everywhere

but the heart wouldn't be found
and everyone was sad

The heart lived for the moment,
we thought, and we said,

the heart was born to be wild
But we were wrong again

Then everyone was furious
with the heart

(as if that was going to help)

Meantime
that ribcage still swung about

empty empty empty

and everyone wouldn't meet
everyone else's eye

and that appeared to be that
until the heart decided otherwise

      Only the heart
      knows how and when to return

and won't say why
it won't say why

Sleeping the sleep

The everyday night
sleeps the sleep,
lost paper eyes-of-the-city,
shut-eye city,
sleep of its peers
or of a faith school

The everyday night's black rainbows
tip their dosh and dollars
into the banks' pockets
and the Pope's goblin-bead tears
fall into the rough and smooth
of his prayer

I often wake in the night
to see that all my sleep's gone west
for my bedroom's not a sleep-lab
where the white-coats
study me

I watch the *wake*
of my sleep
vanish down the whale-road
of the night
hmm
then I go down through
the unlit house
thinking of how you once said
bears don't die
and of lots of old films I've seen
and forgotten,
Clare's Knee for example,
and of all the Shuttles
of Hampshire
Surrey and Middlesex
(there's not many of us,
count us in the phone book)

I make 2 a.m. tea and toast
in the shabby kitchen
on a winter's night missing
its national treasure of snow

Long ago
wakeful nights like this
used to freak me out
now I don't care
I watch Al Jazeera
or tell the wakeful hour
I know where you live...

But sometimes
on a night like this
there's so much silence in the silence
my childhood flings its arms around me
or runs me along a hallway
hung with swords and sabres
or I'm carrying the past somewhere
in a jewelled goblet filled to the Wagnerian brim
with blood-red wine
I mustn't spill one drop
nor take one sip
till I've carried the goblet to safety
wherever that may be
and my dad dear dad can't save me now
from all this waking and sleeping   can he?

Knights

of the mental fight
    I mean
lord's of imagination's
ever-round table
oaken moon of gathering –
knights and strivers
thought-caparisoned
gauntleted with the word
grails kept in their place
yet worshipped well enough
Aircraftsman Shaw's bivouac in the woods
JCP in a tiny cottage under the Ridge at Corwen
that airless room preserved for the itinerant Rilke
in the Hotel Queen Victoria in Ronda
the castle ramparts
where the weather jousted with him
Ivor Gurney at Toussaints
and cry his two names, warningly, sombrely
Mental knights
are those who go through ordeals
mind-lances clashing
they live they die
then say
now you do it –
where are the foremothers
you will ask
but I dub all my mental knights honorary women

Gurney

A river has its moods
as Gurney knew –

the ambitious
scarpfoot spring

moodswing orchards tucked-in
by the meanders

wayward shape-shifting Severn currents
the strike of the rocks

flowing places
where the boats go   locks

remnants of ancient terraces
making their contribution to the flow

dreamy elvers

springline springing up
in the Silurian sandstone

wayward and moody-as-a-poet river
with silver songs
like him

where he sailed
the widening estuary

river he knew
and loved not like a brother

but like Fred Harvey
the Gloucesters

the spirit of Beethoven

Might

True silence
might tell a tale
or lie to save a life
Darkness might flare
by a bedside
or light close its eye
All might change
if change knew how
as love might curse
if it could
or a house flee
from its own rooms
A wise man
might say nothing
but he won't
nor a dog forsake
its master
A book might know
the answer
at midnight
then burn itself
to ash at dawn
Memory might tell
all it knew
or err on the side of truth
and each uncanny woe
we know
might prefer
a hidden life
of prayer
   it might

The hour sees me

at night
thoughts get quieter
but harder
thoughts rise up
old rotten treasure ships
from the seabed
a library of chained books
at night
thoughts are a body
heavy in your arms
or they are the spurned
these hard thoughts
are the night's way
here they are
stern
sometimes they're foolish
that too
there are hours
this is one
when I imagine
the hour sees me
and I see him
but then I won't look
the steps of the city go up
a long way
then there's too much open space
then a friend who's not
the blood is quite a story
he's the king of Cloak Street
making a come-back
all the time
who can practice
the wicked skill of sleep
while the room
speeds through time like this
and night falls into an eye

like a tear-bomb
everything must be braved
a child knows that
and how many heavens
there are or used to be

British Library

Round we go
the bus and I
Gladstone giving us
his stern twinkly blessing
on a little summer
come from nowhere
and nothing
      dear of it
to kiss-better the long
and beastly winter wounds
the British Library
stretching out
behind us
a great basking lion –
      the library knows
many hands many minds
make light work even
of four subterranean floors
of incunabula
only now and then
does a scholar or a volume
hit *the bonk* –
      and from ground level up
the zillion books of life
even the most gadfly of tomes
are sleeping or waking
in their alphabetical lofts
St Pancras
blushing nearby
      only the river
      keeping his cool
      the river
      the bus
         and me

Fools Day

There are so many of us
it takes all morning
to count us
and then the tally may be wrong
of the fools of us
A hand very foolish
comes out of a heart
looking for its chance
A heart very foolish
offers itself to all
unaware
that tricks will be played
A fool looks round
here and there
can't see of course
the *kick-me* sign
stuck on her back
wonders why she ouches
over and again
The strangers-here-themselves
also fall into traps
the buses play dead
so the fools can't go home
the fools are everywhere
just like an ordinary day
Fools Day not so different a day
after all
despite the chalk-white hearts
despite the scuffed seat-of-her-pants
despite the run on the bank
just kidding

Waitrose

In Waitrose Balham
no time to shop
or think about Verdi
no time at all
time's pushing everything
& everyone aside
       move!
taking all the money
all the stuff
In Waitrose Balham
I'm sure I'm bust
and broke
past my sell-by
and my splendour
eye to eye with the floor
heart to heart
with the freezer
left for lost
as Time sweeps through
Waitrose
price-gun in hand
setting an example
hard to follow
Balham clocks unsure
if they're going
forward
or back
lovely silly clocks
by hook or by London crook
waiting so long at the checkout

Shardology

Shardology means
loving its own line of beauty
pyramidal
liking the way Shard
links earth and sky
like a sage of ancient China
and how it tease-floats the eye
over the city's pitch and toss
over its unruly members
lion-faced pageant of London
all its tongue-poker faces
if you're any kind of Shardologist
you'll love the way
it magics and mysteries London
even on a rubbish day like today
no day of days for visiting The Shard
rainy misty murky day
Shard loomy and lost in cloud
fog-straitened sky-capped Shard
no view from you today
you remote rain-pocked pedestal
your obelisk edges
grey-damp to the eye
poor Shard weathery and forlorn
counting your blessings won't work today
Cinderella of the rain
no one's goal
but hey – a true Shardologist
loves Shard in all weathers
this wet-worn Shard
is another sort of lovely –

> cloud-beheaded
> chopped-down to size
> but watch this space
> London
> when the sun shines!

Dug-up roads

What do you hope for
or dream of
or dread
24/7
in the traffic pound
the crazy cloud city
shlock-glass of skyward towers
hip to the max
heartless of course
stomping the city down
under steel hooves
might you not want
to take any more of the same old shit?
what do you hope for?
can you read the streets
hugging their names to their chests
pocket-size churches
slunk in for comfort
every minute of world
stuck fast to them
roads sawn open like cadavers
by the hard-hats?
but highways aren't dead
they're the life
what do you hope for
or think about
these dozed-open streets?

I hope not one person in London
looks down
into such a spoilage today
without feeling
well this is wrong

I took a holiday from my heart

I took a holiday
from my heart

my heart
took a holiday from me

> who was the happier?
> who the wiser?

That first evening
I missed my heart like crazy

always so headstrong
such a show-off

kissing the good life
goodbye

but next morning
I went travelling

Cadiz Kirkuk
Jericho Hanoi

cities
where you don't need a heart

Stupid heart
I said
you won't be seeing me again
any time soon

And no doubt many of us
behave like this
where the heart is concerned

telling our wild-at-heart hearts
to piss off
don't come crawling home
expecting me to

      stuff like that

Heart what more

Heart
what more can I say
we've been here before
cocktails
an iron-glove evening
none finer
what more can be said
when all night it snoweth like ghosts
and you feign the truth
as if you knew more than the north wind
Heart
when we were young
we believed we'd be ashes one day
and now we are
Heart
we've been here before
dancing in a decorated tent
since the beginning
of the world
what more can I say
to you
heartsink heart
I don't blame you Heart
now not a hot coal
though you hacked me all to pieces then
nor never yet conceived me
lying in wait for me
again and again
like a little clot or seam or patch
in the air
when the spider decides
to be gentle

Girls in Bristol

Why so sad
you girls in The Old Duke
where ghosts play snipsnap jazz

you girls in the riverside cafes
on buses crossing The Downs

or in the shopping slipstreams
of Cabot Circus and Cribb's Causeway?

Why so many sad-eyed girls
in Bristol where story-voices speak

tales and mysteries
to uncripple the lonely and find the lost

and help the sad eyes learn better –
forget-me-not tales

for girls hanging in there
not letting a teardrop fall   not one

I wonder why
and I wonder if a big quiet river

helps sad girls and others
maybe in simple ways

thousands of little answers
many kinds of light and shade

so broken hearts can go breezing along
by the river that wishes them well

whispering
wanna a cuddle, sweetie?

and this feels okay   sometimes –
then   night falls

on the Mild Mild West at Stokes Cross
on The Grim Reaper and The Flying Fortress

night falls along Gloucester Road
and down Bread Street

on that old pet shop in Bedminister
and on a bragging Park Street fool...

      the saxophone sees
      where all this is going

      the vodka drinker
      lines 'em up

Buses take the weary home
along countless roads of houses

criss-crossing countless roads of houses
as if everyone in the world

lived in this one city   *they don't*
houses bend the knee

fire stations and police cars
rock themselves to sleep

The Orpheus counts its rats
above Waitrose in Henleaze

And too soon a tomorrow comes
but get up sad girl

get showered dressed
eat breakfast catch the bus go to work

in broken-heart Bristol
where the river dips and dives

its local shifts of light
tides flex their big muscles

and the harbourside
will champion my sad girl

like a knight of yore
Gawain or Lancelot

or dear dear Sir Bedivere

Shardologist

I want to live up here
head in the clouds
speaking in tongues
from this Babel
(but in a good way) Tower
I need to live in the sunny uplands
of my beautiful Shard
Her Grace of London Bridge
a stone's throw away
from the Bridge Master
(I like to think of him fashioning
a tiny house out of the fragments of his own skin
given to him post-op
just as I like to think
of The Mayor in his lesser palace
dress-making and dream-making
the hours away
a bee-hive in his mouth)
Shard
glassy obelisk
smarting with morning dew
Shard
standing tall
in your 72 floor cloak of visibility
far-below-Thames
marvels at itself become so titchy
a brook a stream
Buck House tiny
Southwark Cathedral tinier
Wembley Stadium tiniest
teeny-weeny Borough Market
under its fingernail
of green roof
bridges made of spider-thread
the urban pan of the horizon scooped out far away to the London
     Array –

The Shard is where I want to live
to be Shard poet in residence
or the Shard's stowaway
Shard's sisterling
my bag's already packed
because
I'm a born Shardologist
                    of course

Osmium

A piece of Osmium about the size of a paper grocery bag
weighs as much as a new car, a small Honda Accord,
for instance...

Some years are light
as air
you don't even have to lift them
from your memory
they float their weightless goodies
in and out of your today
with less fuss
than a summer cloud roaming the sky

but other years
are heavy as a suitcase full of a murdered torso
heavier than plutonium or osmium
darker than ten thousand leagues under the sea –
you need the strongest crane in the world
(if indeed the technology of lifting
is advanced enough even today)
to raise one such year into plain sight –

                                                    dead weight –

so perhaps don't try
let those behemoth years lie

drive away quick in your little red Honda

New Ceramics Galleries

(V and A)

Do not bring your bull
into this china shop
leave your backpack in the cloakroom
the ten thousand things of ceramics
are here
perfect silence of shepherd and shepherdess
crafted from hands of old potters
unfrequented galleries
where you hear the empty vessels
singing the song of untouchability itself
in a deep atmosphere of retreat and inwardness
as if we're ten thousand leagues under the sea
oh decorative and reticent silence of the ceramic galleries
containing pure cup pure bowl pure handle ten thousand times over
ten thousand lids and lips and bowls and vases
and saucers and egg rings and great ewers
in phalanxes and regiments and rows
of perfect porcelain
so many silent cups
empty plates
bowls reaching for the sky
a set of blue and white porringers
but no Goldilocks invited
no bears
each bowl contains merely a portion of air
the repast of silence
no riposte to my questioning gaze
a trove too beauteous for its own good
wares drawn from the muck of earth and fire –
dinner plates side plates coffee cups
tear-bottles snuff-bottles sauce-boats candlesticks
patterned painted tiles
like cards of a thousand tarot packs
punchbowls and pickle dishes
and terrines glazed to a tee

big enough to feed an army
but they're buried alive
like the funerary hoard of the greatest monarch ever
or the chattels of Sleeping Beauty
fallen under a spell
never touched
not a plate or cup flung across a room
in a fine fierce marital dispute
they've been put on pause for ever and a day
prisoned in glass cabinets stretching into infinity
like a motionless hunger march
but no one will be fed –
or maybe all of this is God's china cabinet?
for here's an Adam and Eve dinner service
in bold rough clunky colours of green and gold and red
the servile sullen pair clad
in animal skins
and nearby the snake is smiling

Bitch

His handbones
check out
of the Metropole
the finest hotel in Belgium
his Richard the Third limbs
rise and fall from
strength to strength
Speaking thoughts turn to him
and finish alone
so he runs his own gauntlet
now and then
His throat's quiet
like a big room split at the seams
Hours smite him
and the peacock on his back
but he lives for some other kind
of daylight
his pocket a gig at the Hippodrome
his eyes scooping me in
for good or ill
yep I'm done for
damn blast
and darn it
I'm his

We or I

We or I don't know
how near the day is
or not
when a word
will ask so much of us or me
ask who made
all this sad stuff
of the world
these buildings these cities
these people
in their quest or prison
we or I don't know if
a word
will hold us or me
and not let us go
if it holds me or us
for one minute
that will be the end of us
or you
unless an answer
comes from the deep place
of answers
unless we or I find it
that day is not near
but far
perhaps it will be the night
not the day
that speaks
or will silence blurt us or me
into the vineyard
into the vintage
into the gob of the street?

lol

no one
turns the page
or treads the stair
the house sighs
when the sea winds blow
and how they blow
like country 'n' western
emotions cheap and sure
no one rests his head
or laughs out loud
the room's full of
another evening's light
blinds undrawn at eight
the chairs exactly aligned
the radio is echoes
of many days
of a quiet moment
found at the back
of everything

a week or so later
you hear a tune
that knows its song
too well
the tune
for no one drinking
a glass of whiskey or wine
or water
the drinker
with seeing eyes
lingers the afternoon away
the shaken world
is no place to be
on a day like this
so far away
like a school
for the indignant blind

Opposite

The opposite of day
is night
and moonlight
is a kind of convenience store
for moths
and crickets
and the sleepless

The opposite of water
is beer
but in Okhotsk
they make a beer
called Okhotsk Blue
using melt water from icebergs

The opposite of air
is earth
and tucked in the earth
there's a vast underground ocean
three times greater
than all the seas we know
there it is
trapped in the molecular structure
of minerals
within the mantle rock
taking a form that is neither liquid
nor ice nor vapour
but spongily living its curious life
at the earth's hot heart

The opposite of food
is sleep
and also dreaming
where anyone can move
between this world
and that of the gods and heroes –
here I find it helps to think

that a python sleeps eighteen hours
out of twenty four
an African elephant sleeps
3.3 hours
and a giraffe a mere 1.9

The opposite of sense
is nonsense
which never writes its will
or a love letter or a prize-winning essay
but is never bored
and exists
(who can doubt it?)
in its own bright heartfelt truth
like the stars themselves
who are the opposite of telling lies
sparkling night and day
up there in the sky
with never a word of thanks
from god or man

Alone

is not the point
nor the reason
Alone is full of life
hard as stone
clear as water
old as time
Alone is feeling the heat
bends low
at your feet
like a queen
Alone is the day
quick with light
the midnight absolute
Some of this is the point
but not all of it
is the point
If there's a wise place
alone is not it
nor the cloud of hours
nor the day's green hand
Alone is very safe
or so it seems
and stars are masters of it
I walk a little faster
Alone comes along
like no lover I've ever known
and here's a day
the same backwards
as forwards
clouds lose their way
meetings get stuck
in the middle
cities unsteady their nerves
the Lidls and the Asdas
chain their eyes to the floor
my scrap of time asks why

I answer
but to no one
the owned unowned air
holds its breath
the day's a puzzle
to itself
no one has seen it begin
no one knows how to end it
no one knows why alone is always here
to lend a helpless hand

Maybe

a year can be
just what's needed
toting its days
as a cloud its night
fresh from the dark
a year might throw
light on everything
who knows
so that all is known
and understood
that would be nice
or a year
might fail to please
not ever wish
to please
a year involves so much
is it worth trying again
the year won't say
this week goes by
that week goes by
nothing waits
fields rush
into their green aisles
a raindrop closes
the door
words fail me
a year could change all that
let's go into this café
shall we
let's do something
the day won't wait
the roads attend their lords
a year is finding its feet
I wait and hurry
no doubt the year schemes me on
a day fetches me out of there

a window says
peace be upon you
but I'm not sure
I'm not sure

Heart

heart was alone
as heart preferred
the day went on
as heart commanded
rain stood quietly
by the window
waiting for heart
to notice
   no dice
heart was too busy
too alone
as heart preferred
as heart commanded
when heart got tired
the day ended
and when I spoke
heart didn't answer
heart never answered –
all night heart admired the dark
heart almost loved the dark
at break of day
heart ached just a little
like any old heart
but wouldn't change
not even for Joseph's
collar of gold

heart stood alone
as heart preferred
as heart commanded
holding heart's woe
in a glass darkly

NOTES

Chagall (17) incorporates adapted quotations from writings on and by Chagall. Chagall writes:

> To my city Vitebsk:
> Why? Why did I leave you many years ago?... You thought, the boy seeks something, seeks such a special subtlety, that colour descending like stars from the sky and landing, bright and transparent, like snow on our roofs. Where did he get it? How would it come to a boy like him? I don't know why he couldn't find it with us, in the city – in his homeland. Maybe the boy is 'crazy', but 'crazy' for the sake of art... You thought: 'I can see, I am etched in the boy's heart, but he is still "flying", he is still striving to take off, he has "wind" in his head'... I did not live with you, but I didn't have one single painting that didn't breathe with your spirit and reflection.

Will You Walk a Little Faster? (20): The city is Oxford. The title is from 'The Lobster Quadrille' by Lewis Carroll: 'Will you walk a little faster / said a whiting to a snail / there's a porpoise close behind us / and he's treading on my tail.'

Along the great moon (43): Alain Robert is the grand-daddy of all urban climbers but was prevented by security guards from ascending The Shard while it was in construction.

little Monday (56): For the neologism 'omday' I'm indebted to the late Linda Helen Smith.

Passages (68): I'm indebted to the artist Andrea Maclean for the inspiration of her work and for her talk 'Visionary Cartography' at Ledbury Poetry Festival in 2010. I'm also indebted to the work of the artist Margaret Jarvis.

Knights (79): JCP is John Cowper Powys. *'and cry his two names, warningly, sombrely'*: a quotation from 'It is Near Toussaints' by Ivor Gurney.

Gurney (80): I am indebted for some geographical details here to *Ivor Gurney's Gloucestershire* by Eleanor Rawlings.

Girls in Bristol (92): The Orpheus is a cinema in the Henleaze district of Bristol. The Mild Mild West, the Grim Reaper, and the Flying Fortress are the names of works of street art in Bristol.